A Collection
of
Advent Readings

Lindsay Mizell

The King is Coming: A Collection of Advent Readings, Maryville Vineyard Church Edition

Available from Amazon.com, CreateSpace.com, and other retail outlets.

This title is also available as an ebook.

Requests for information should be addressed to:
Maryville Vineyard Church, 713 William Blount Drive, Maryville, TN 37801

Cover: Lindsay Mizell & Matt Farrand
Back Cover: Jon Pemberton
Editor: Sarah Small
Interior: Matt Farrand

FOR NANNY

who smells like Jesus

Says a country legend told every year:
Go to the barn on Christmas Eve and see
what the creatures do as that long night tips over.
Down on their knees they will go, the fire
of an old memory whistling through their minds!
I went. Wrapped to my eyes against the cold
I creaked back the barn door and peered in.

-from "Christmas Poem" by Mary Oliver

A Welcome...

The Fall has been long and hard and I have been longing for this journey. Longing for a chance to lean forward and for 26 days to look deeply and intentionally into the great rescue. Longing for a quiet heart to wait and watch for the coming of the True King. Longing for something deeper than I have dared to dive into.

Thank you for daring to join me. Find your spot and something warm to drink. Light a candle or the tree, and take a breath. We will not travel lightly. The road will be rocky and words will fail, but even still, the King will come.

He will always come...

How to use this Book

I was way too old before I really understood how to have a "quiet time." No one really talks about the ins and the outs of spending time with Jesus. Here are my thoughts on the matter. This book is divided up into 26 devotional readings. Each day will have the same three things:

- Scripture—a set of verses for the day, some new and some you will see over and over again.
- Reading—some thoughts on the verses and how they impact our lives this season and lots of quotes from people way smarter than me.
- Prayer—stolen from songs and saints, a few words to pray and reflect to end your time.

The most effective way to read this book is to find a time each day that works for you. The time will not just happen; it is something that needs to be intentionally carved out and initiated. Basically, you will never accidentally have a quiet time. I am still trying to prove this wrong, with no success. Find a time and a place that is quiet. Then, grab your bible and a pen. Turn on the Spotify playlist from the back if it is helpful. There are some good tunes in there.

My favorite way to start is to take a breath and try and calm down my mind. This might sound strange, but I just need a minute to sit and to be and to get rid of the 7 million thoughts plaguing my brain. Then, start every day with the selected verses. In a lot of ways, I hope you never get past them. I hope that they captivate you and breathe life and hope into you. When you have read the verses, take another minute to pause and to think. There are many ways to do this. I normally spend time thinking about each of these questions:

- What is God saying about himself?
- What is God saying about/to this world?
- What is God saying about/to me?

There are some lines provided if you want to jot down some thoughts. I am a journaler and I need this chance to write down what I hope not to forget. In a way, this book is a glance into my journal and personal thoughts about these scriptures. You don't have to write it in the book. You can write it on a post-it or a computer or on your hand. You can draw pictures in the margins. Do what is life-giving to you.

The next step is to read the reading for the day. You may want to journal or write or draw some after. And finally, when you are done reading and you are done responding, the prayer at the bottom is a great final step. It is good on its own and it is good as a opening to your own prayers.

Again, thanks for joining me in this. What an adventure!

A Collection of Advent Readings

Day 1

Scripture: 1 Peter 1:8-13

Advent feels like a sweet memory peeled back slowly. Layer by layer. Petal by petal.

The Greek word for advent is parousia, meaning "coming." For hundreds of years the people of God have spent four Sundays and the days in between intentionally preparing themselves for what was and for what is to come. Hundreds of years of candles and readings. The saints before us have paved a long and rich history of preparation.

And yet, I always miss it.

I always have good intentions—intentions to prepare, to heed the warnings: Christmas is easy to miss in tinsel and trimming. But, if we are not careful, we can also miss it in the familiar. Stories and carols roll off our tongues, warm and known. The familiar winks at busy and rushing and tense. Familiar has a tendency to overshadow the magic.

This year, I want the magic.

Advent is the invitation to creak back the barn door and to watch the magic unfold. It will unfold in the candles, the questions of children, the wine and the wheat, the twinkling lights and the benevolence of strangers and saints. But more than anywhere, it will unfold in the magic of the ancient words sent from the

Holy Spirit in the scriptures. As we set our hope fully on the grace they offer, we must dig deeper into the familiar, exposing the adventure and the magic and the rescue of the parousia.

Prayer:

Come and stand amazed, you people,
See how God is reconciled!
See his plans of love accomplished,
See his gift, this newborn child.
See the Mighty, weak and tender,
See the Word who now is mute.
See the Sovereign without splendor,
See the Fullness destitute;
The Beloved, whom we covet,
In a state of low repute.

-from the medieval Dutch carol "Come and Stand Amazed"

Day 2

Scripture: Isaiah 7:10-24

My boys have a plastic nativity set. It has what feels like a thousand pieces and a battery-operated star that shines and sings and announces the nearness of God. And it drives me crazy. My boys lose the pieces and they push the button to turn on the star at all of the wrong times. And the God of the plastic nativity seems to take on a trivial nearness.

> *For those who claim his name, Christmas heralds this luminous truth: The God of Jesus Christ is our absolute future. Such is the deeply hopeful character of this sacred season. By God's free doing in Bethlehem, nothing can separate us from the love of God in Christ Jesus. Light, life and love are on our side.*
>
> -Brennan Manning

The song of the plastic nativity is the song of the scriptures. Yet, it is the song that for many of us has become too familiar, too easy to swallow. Though it has been gift wrapped and under-realized, it is truly the song of the ages, the luminous truth. The song declaring that God would come to this world and that nothing could separate us from him. He is near because the veil would be lifted and nothing would stand between. The nearness is not trivial. It is magical. The music will find its way to our ears at every turn this season, from the plastic nativity to the mall to the candle-lit service on Christmas Eve: God demands our response, over and over again.

This luminous truth will lead us to great adventures this season. It will take us to grand and terrifying places. But, the mountains and the valleys will lead us toward a stable where a King will come. A king who is our future, our hope, our light and life and love.

Prayer:

O God, our Luminous Truth, do not let us miss the adventure. Do not let us miss your promise and your rescue in the regular and the trivial. May we find you near in the notes that feel familiar. May our ears burn with your truth over and over and over again until it becomes the very song of our heart. Amen.

Day 3

Scripture: Genesis 3

The story does not begin in a stable under the brightest star. Instead, the story begins long before. In a quiet garden. A garden that was perfect in community, made for a man and his wife and the One who spun them into being.

If I am honest I wish that preparing my heart for Christmas to come would not mean looking closer into this garden. It is the story none of us long to tell—the story of how from the first bite of the juiciest apple, everything changed.

To look into that garden in a true way means that we must look into our own garden, full of our own apples. Our own choices and secrets. Our own passivity and our own aggression. Our obsession with ourselves. Our quest for perfection and pleasure. It means that we must look at Adam and look at Eve, sure that if it was us in that perfect garden, we would have done the exact same thing. Our hands would have wrapped the fruit, our mouths watering at its promise of knowledge and power and control.

To prepare our hearts for Christmas, we must be brave enough to stare into the darkness.

The people who walked in darkness
have seen a great light;
those who dwelt in a land of deep darkness,
on them has light shone.

-Isaiah 9:2

We, who long for what is easy, what can be controlled, what will numb and please—have spent our days walking and dwelling in the darkness. And He, who longs to rescue and redeem and restore—has shone a great light.

The king is coming...

Prayer:

O Lord, The house of my soul is narrow; enlarge it that you may enter in. It is ruinous, O repair it! It displeases Your sight. I confess it, I know. But who shall cleanse it, to whom shall I cry but to you? Cleanse me from my secret faults, O Lord, and spare Your servant from strange sins. Amen.
-St. Augustine

Day 4

Scripture: Isaiah 53:1-12

In the same way Advent does not begin in a stable, it does not end in a garden. The good news is that even though we all have gone astray, apple in our hand and control in our eyes, the story is only just beginning.

> *And though they would forget him, and run from him, deep in their hearts, God's children would miss him always, and long for him—lost children yearning for their home.*
>
> *Before they left the garden, God whispered a promise to Adam and Eve: "It will not always be so! I will come to rescue you! And when I do, I'm going to do battle against the snake. I'll get rid of the sin and the dark and the sadness you let in here. I'm coming back for you!"*
>
> *And he would. One day, God himself would come.*
>
> -The Jesus Storybook Bible

If the news of the season is true, you can never be the same. If God himself came, then the longing for something more can be filled. The fruit will always look appealing. Your mind will wander and your feet will run. But, you were never meant to live in the empty longing of the apple. You have always been meant to prosper in the hand of the Lord. God himself came to fight a battle to bring you home. Whatever it looks like for you and wherever you are, this is the season to come back home.

Prayer:

Behold, Lord, an empty vessel that needs to be filled. My Lord, fill it. I am weak in the faith; strengthen me. I am cold in love; warm me and make me fervent, that my love may go out to my neighbor. I do not have a strong and firm faith; at times I doubt and am unable to trust you altogether. O Lord, help me. Strengthen my faith and trust in you. In you I have sealed the treasure of all I have. I am poor; you are rich and came to be merciful to the poor. I am a sinner; you are upright. With me, there is an abundance of sin; in you is the fullness of righteousness. Therefore I will remain with you, of whom I can receive, but to whom I may not give. Amen.

-Martin Luther

Day 5

Scripture: Isaiah 8:5-17

Immanuel. In Isaiah and Matthew, the prophecy finds a name. A baby will be born and he will be called Immanuel. God with us.

God would come to rescue and to save and to put back together. But he would also come near. He would come in community and in intimacy. He would come near as a sanctuary for the hearts of the terrified, the lonely, the broken. The God of the universe came to earth to be with us. With us in our triumphs and when all of it falls apart. With us in the moments we never could dream of and with us the moments we never knew to dread. God with us, our comfort and the battle cry of our hearts.

> *Put me on the wild ocean, and let my ship dance madly on the waves; I would still say, "Immanuel, God with us." Mount me on the sunbeam, and let me fly beyond the western sea; still I would say, "God with us." Let my body dive down into the depths of the ocean, and let me hide in its caverns; still I could, as a child of God, say, "God with us."*
>
> *-C.H. Spurgeon*

You are not alone. Immanuel is near.

Prayer:

Oh Immanuel, oh God with us.
Our Deliverer, You are Savior.
In Your presence
we find our strength over everything.
You are our redemption. You are God with us.
You are here, You are holy.
And we are standing in Your glory.
Amen.

-adapted from the song "God With Us" by All Sons & Daughters

Day 6

Scripture: Isaiah 53:7-12; Jeremiah 31:1-4

The coming of Jesus changes everything. He came, not only to be with us, he also came for us. Because only through him only could we ever be rescued. Through him only could we ever be rebuilt. For thousands of years God gave the Israelites hints of a Savior. Promises, whispered and trumpeted, that there was a plan.

The coming of Jesus changes everything. He was willing and able to step into what we destroyed with our own two hands. He was the One, the Holy, who could put it all back together again. No matter how great the damage or how deep the wounds, his rescue is greater still. No matter how patiently or impatiently you have waited, or how deeply you believe. His rescue is greater than us and beyond us and for us. You have not been left in your rubble.

The story of Christmas is the story of the world being rebuilt. The child came to be with you and the child came for you. He is your grace in the wilderness, your rest in a far away place. He loves you with an everlasting love. And He, only He, can build you up.

Oh yes, the words of old are still true today: You shall be built.

Prayer:

For your mercies' sake, O Lord my God, tell me what you are to me. Say to my soul: "I am your salvation." So speak that I may hear, O Lord. My heart is listening; open it that it may hear you, and say to my soul: "I am your salvation." After hearing this word, may I come in haste to take hold of you. Hide not your face from me. Let me see your face even if I die, lest I die with longing to see it. The house of my soul is too small to receive you; let it be enlarged by you. It is all in ruins; do you repair it. There are things in it - I confess and I know - that must offend your sight. But who shall cleanse it? Or to what others besides you shall I cry out? From my secret sins cleanse me, O Lord, and from those of others spare your servant. Amen.

-St. Augustine

Day 7

Scripture: Isaiah 61:1-11

It is not finding the Immanuel in the holiday that is difficult, rather the difficulty lies in what happens when we find him. Because if his coming was to be with us and for us, that will change things inside and outside of us. Brennan Manning calls those who dare to "celebrate as if he is near" the "victorious minority." If God came near, there are great risks to be taken.

But only the victorious dare to take them.

Believing that in this moment the Holy has come near will make us choose an awkward apology in a long devastated relationship. It will dare us to measure the heart of our giving against the heart of the great Giver. To celebrate by diving deeply into the messes of the brokenhearted and the captives, speaking words of hope into the darkness. It means having loving enough to be honest and brave enough to wander into deeper territory. It is engaging when we want to retreat, walking when our legs are tired, and speaking when the words are hard to find. It is taking notice of the empty seats and plates and stockings. Celebrating as if God really came near will require more from us than we could ever imagine.

And yet, we will never go alone. In the awkward and the risk and the uncomfortable, the battle cry of our hearts remains the same: "God with us!"

Prayer:

Lord God, You have appointed me...
But you see how unsuited I am to meet so great and difficult a task. If I had lacked Your help, I would have ruined everything long ago. Therefore, I call upon You: I wish to devote my mouth and my heart to you. Use me as Your instrument—but do not forsake me, for if ever I should be on my own, I would easily wreck it all. Amen.

-Martin Luther

Day 8

Scripture: Isaiah 11:1-5; 12:1-6

The magic of this season will lie in the moments we devote to waiting and watching for Him to come. He will still come if our hearts are loud and our days are busy and our eyes are distracted. But there is magic to be found in the intentional moments of quiet, with our eyes and hearts taking notice of what has come. There is magic when we dare to celebrate as if he is near.

This season fills each of our senses with gifts: sights, sounds, things to smell and touch and taste. But, as Augustine reminds us, the gifts must not terminate on themselves. Rather, they fill us with the glory and the praise and the worship of the most true Giver. He has filled this season with holy moments of nearness. Moments when you stand still in the middle of a room, full of those you love most, listening as his song bellows in the laughter and glad tidings. He will be near in the wonder and magic of the hearts of children anxiously awaiting the beard and the belly of St. Nick, whose story sets the stage of the greater benevolence of the perfect Giver. The twinkling lights strung in long lines will announce the hope of the Immanuel. The smells and the sounds of every store and home will be the aroma of the One who will put all things back together. In these moments when we choose to pause long enough notice His nearness, we will hear the whispers of our own stories as they are grafted into the greatest story.

Prayer:

I will give thanks to you, O Lord,
for though you were angry with me your anger turned away, that you might comfort me.
You are my salvation.
I will trust and I will not be afraid,
for you are my strength and my song.
I will thank you and I will call upon you.
I will stand on the roof tops and declare what you have done for me.
And the earth will cry, "Glory!"
For you are the giver of all good things.
Amen.

-from Isaiah 12

Day 9

Scripture: John 1:1-4

Since the beginning, there has only been one story...

The great rescue of the father, told since the beginning of time, began in the Garden. We fell and experienced the great sadness and separation that declared need of our rescue. For hundreds of years, the Lord declared his promise: in the wind and the waves, on the tongues of the prophets and in the belly of a whale, in covenants, on mountaintops, in the colors of a rainbow and the slinging of a stone. Over and over and over again the story was told. Until it was quiet. And in the silence, earth held its breath and waited.

For 400 years the people of Israel wandered in the desert and waited. They committed themselves to the Law, constantly aware that they would never measure up. They relished the words of the prophets, clinging to the promise of a rescue. They tried to grasp the voice of their maker but the silence was deafening. As the years passed and new generations were born, the promises became harder to hear and even silly to believe. But still, in the deathly quiet, they waited.

And then, after 400 years of total silence, the word came.

Jesus. The word that broke the silence and it began the story. The story that breaks through the quiet and breathes life into our dead and dark places. The story of hope and the story of rescue. The story that is worth waiting for, even when it feels like forever.

The story always comes...

Prayer:

In a world of created changeable things,
Christ and his Word alone remain unshaken.
O to forsake all creatures,
to rest as a stone on him the foundation,
to abide in him, be borne up by him!
For all my mercies come through Christ,
who has designed, purchased, promised,
effected them.
How sweet it is to be near him, the Lamb.
O thou who has the hearts of all men in thine hand,
from my heart according to the Word,
according to the image of thy Son,
so shall Christ the Word, and his Word,
be my strength and comfort.
Amen.

-adapted from "Christ the Word," Valley of Vision

Day 10

Scripture: Luke 1:5-25

> *A reasonable human question receives an answer that exceeds all human reason. It exceeds, too, the natural law. But the angel turns from rules to the Ruler. He grounds the truth of his answer not in creation but in the Creator, whose word shall never be impossible.*
>
> -Walter Wangerin Jr.

Elizabeth and Zechariah never saw it coming. Luke describes them as righteous followers. And then, he calls her barren. The word has a tendency to define those it claims. And the word, it doesn't come alone. It lives in the shadows of words like "empty" and "impossible."

But the angel turns from the rules to the Ruler...

The unbelievable became true and the impossible started growing in an old woman's belly. Suddenly what was empty had been filled with the miracle of a God who had chosen the Way. And what had been silent inside of her was filled with laughter and joy and a thankfulness that had been hidden, waiting in her bones.

And behold, your relative Elizabeth in her old age has also conceived a son, and this is the sixth month with her who was called barren. For nothing will be impossible with God.

-Luke 1:36-37

The God who filled her womb removed the word that defined her. In defiance of nature and the laws of medicine, the Ruler blew life into the empty places. For him, nothing is impossible. No place is too dark, too broken, too empty. The truth of this season is that in all of our pain and our doubt, our fear and anger, and our broken and empty places.

The king is coming.

Prayer:

Lord, in the daytime stars can be seen from deepest wells, and the deeper the wells the brighter thy stars shine; Let me find thy light in my darkness, thy life in my death, thy joy in my sorrow, thy grace in my sin, thy riches in my poverty, thy glory in my valley. Amen.

-Valley of Vision

Day 11

Scripture: Luke 1:25-45

The story of Mary and the angel takes place within the ultimate equation of the scriptures. The pages are full of stories about before and after. Stories where the world or person or kingdom operates in a certain way and then a few little words come and completely change the trajectory of the story. Conjunction words like "but god" and "therefore," offering a picture of before and after, are found over 3,000 times in scripture. All of our favorite stories are full of these conjunctions, promises bridging the former and now to prepare a way for the miraculous. A small boy turned into a hero with only a few stones. A man terrified to speak who became the leader of all of Israel. A man and woman banished and reconciled in the same chapter. Stories that many of us have heard our entire lives. Stories that Mary knew. There is a deep value in knowing the stories.

There she was, unwed and unprepared. Young and terrified in the face of an angel. Greatly troubled at his choice of words and unable to understand what they could mean. And then...THEREFORE. One word to bridge the before and the after: her fears and her questions to the promise of the Holy.

And everything changed.

"I belong to the Lord, body and soul," replied Mary. "Let it happen as you say." And at this the angel left her.

-Luke 1:38, JB Phillips

The stable is full of stories of a God who intervenes. A God who enters the impossible and creates a way where there could never be one. The stable is a picture of his promise to make rivers in the wasteland and to bring grace in the wilderness and fill the empty places of our world and our hearts.

Just when it could never be true, there is a timely placed conjunction and the "therefore" changes everything.

Prayer:

Oh Lord, that I would belong to you body and soul. That I would learn to see and trust in you, the God who intervenes in order to make rescue. Be the river in my wasteland, the grace in my wilderness. Fill my empty places that I might believe. And in my belief, give me the faith and the courage to mutter the words "Let it happen as you say." Amen.

Day 12

Scripture: Luke 1:46-56

Mary's Prayer, the *Magnificat*. Theologian NT Wright calls it "the gospel before the gospel." It is the spoken celebration of a mother exploding with joy over the birth of her child. It is the song and dance of an Israelite who has only known a lifetime of waiting. It is the words of a woman, who believes body and soul that there is a rescue. It is a song of praise from the lips of someone who has been noticed by the God of the Universe.

In these words Mary sings the song of our deliverance. The song of our rescue. The song that claims we have been noticed. For, this Magnificat is our song as well.

The gospel before the gospel.

The stable is God's proof that you have been remembered. The Holy has looked on you and he has noticed. He has come and he comes bringing mercies to pile on his people.

> *His mercy flows in wave after wave*
> *on those who are in awe before him.*
>
> -Luke 1:50, The Message

You, who feel alone in a crowded room. You, who can barely read the words of this song, and certainly cannot utter them. You, who wonder if anyone notices. You, who feel unsatisfied and underappreciated and unknown. You, who think you have gone to far. You, who are pretending to have it all together. You, who are reading these words.

You have not been forgotten.

The king is coming.

Prayer:

My heart is overflowing with praise of my Lord, my soul is full of joy in God my Saviour. For, you have noticed me. You, the one who can do all things, has done great things for me—oh, holy is your Name! Your mercy rests on those who follow you. You are the help of Israel, my only help today. You remembered Israel, wandering in the desert for so many years. And you have remembered me, with a mercy that flows in wave after wave. You are the good news that overflows from every crevice and cavern on this earth and in my heart. You have not forgotten me. Amen.

Day 13

Scripture: Luke 1:57-79

Augustine says that the birth of John the Baptist is the boundary between the Old Testament and the New Testament. A picture of the old and the new, literally born to elderly parents, barren and longing, mute and doubting. And in a few short verses, a mother and a righteous follower and a new life coming to prepare the way for what is to come. The barrier between the prophets and the law and the Savior who would fulfill it all.

John calls himself, "the voice of the one crying out in the wilderness." His job as the barrier is to belt one cry to all who would listen: He is coming. The king is coming. Prepare the way for him. What John the Baptist offers Israel, many have offered us. Voices crying out to us, calling us toward the Word who was and is the always. The saints who stand as barriers between the before and the after. In my life there have been so many voices calling to me, stuck in the darkness of a wild and barren land. Voices daring me toward the Holy.

In this season the voices continue to cry. The king is coming. Prepare the way. It is not too late. It is not too late to prepare the way for Christmas to come, in our homes and in our hearts. It is not too late to see, for the first time or the thousandth, the ways we have neglected his coming in our lives. It is not too late to find the One who changes everything in the midst of the things we think are important. It is not too late to let the words of Zechariah, proclaiming the voice of his Son, to seep into our busy minds and wandering hearts:

> *"...because of the tender mercy of our God,*
> *whereby the sunrise shall visit us from on high*
> *to give light to those who sit in darkness and in the shadow of death,*
> *to guide our feet into the way of peace."*
>
> -Luke 1:78-79

Prayer:

> *No human mind could ever conceive or invent the gospel. Acting in eternal grace, you are both its messenger and its message, lived out on earth through infinite compassion, applying your life to insult, injury, death, that I might be redeemed, ransomed, freed. Help me to give up every darling lust, to submit heart and life to its command, to have it in my will, controlling my affections, molding my understanding...Take me to the cross to seek glory from its infamy; strip me of every pleasing pretense of righteousness by doing my own things. O gracious Redeemer, I have neglected thee too long. Amen.*
>
> -from Valley of Vision

Day 14

Scripture: Luke 2:1-5

These words fill me with so much cheer and wonder and magic, "In those days a decree went out from Caesar Augustus…" They transplant me into a full sanctuary that smells of pine and sounds like Christmas carols, peeling last year's dripping wax off of the candle in my hand. Words that for my entire life have announced the coming of the King. Words that I knew by heart before I ever understood. Words that began the story that changed everything.

Words that bring us to Bethlehem and to the manger. Words that invite us to stay a while and look a little bit closer.

> *As for Bethlehem, that blazing star*
> *still sailed the dark, but only looked for me.*
> *Caught in its light, listening again to its story,*
> *I curled against some sleepy breast, who nuzzled*
> *my hair as though I were a child, and warmed me*
> *the best it could all night.*
>
> *-Mary Oliver, Twelve Moons*

Words that meet you no matter where you are and where you have been. Words announcing the beginning of the rescue to those of us who need it terribly and those of us who don't think we need it at all. Words that ask you to pause and consider where you have been and who is coming.

Prayer:

O Holy Spirit, as the sun is full of light, the ocean full of water, heaven full of glory, so may my heart be full of you. Give me eyes to see Jesus and the realities of the unseen world.

Give me yourself without measure, as an unimpaired fountain, as inexhaustible riches.

I bewail my coldness, poverty, emptiness, imperfect vision, lazy service, prayerless prayers, praiseless praises. May I not resist seeing you.

Come as power, to expel every rebellious bone in me, to reign supreme and keep me yours. Come as teacher,leading me into all truth, filling me with all understanding. Come as love, that I may adore the Father, and love him as my all. Come as joy,to dwell in me, move in me, animate me. Come as light, illuminating the Scripture, molding me in its laws. Come as sanctifier, body, soul and spirit wholly yours. Come as helper, with strength to bless and keep, directing my every step. Come as beautifier, bringing order out of confusion, loveliness out of chaos.

Magnify to me your glory by being magnified in me, and make me full of your fragrance. Amen

-adapted from Valley of Vision

Day 15

Scripture: Matthew 1:18-25

It is so easy to look at the characters of this ancient story and to appreciate their brave obedience. Mary and Joseph, willing to walk into the confusing and the embarrassing and the unknown. They hear the voice of the Holy and they listen and obey. Maybe they weighed the pros and the cons. Maybe they considered the risks. But what is clear is that even in their fear and confusion and questions, they trusted the heart of the one who made them and the one who placed this child within them.

It is so easy to look at the Nativity and see its beauty and adventure. But this story demands something more than appreciation; it demands us to respond. We will completely miss the Nativity if our reading it stops at appreciation. The invitation of this story is for our appreciation to move into the deep groan of gratitude. And, from the depths of our groanings, it invites us into action.

Before he was born, Mary and Joseph believed that their son would come to save his people from their sins. It is this belief that makes their obedience brave and not ridiculous. In spite of the hundreds of reasons it seemed crazy, they believed in the story that has been told since the beginning of this world: they would bear a son called Jesus, and he would be the Messiah. And, he is. He is the one that would change everything. All of creation has been groaning for him.

He is the one you have always longed for. He is the only one who will fill you. And all gratitude is for him. And all brave obedience is found through him. And this child is inviting you into the adventure his parents knew well. The Nativity reminds us that we were never meant to live a small life of small obedience. We were meant to live a life of great adventure because we can trust the one who is the Messiah.

Prayer:

> *O God, you are my rescue. You are my strength and refuge. You are my help. I will not be afraid, even if the earth gives way and the mountains fall into the sea. Even though the waters might roar and foam and the mountains may tremble. For, I know that you will come and rescue me. Though kingdoms may rage and nations may fall, your help will come as the dawn comes every morning. For, the earth does whatever you tell it to. And you will come and rescue me. For, you are God. You are exalted over all, majestic over all, stronger than all. And even still, you come and rescue me. Amen.*
>
> -adapted from Psalm 46

Day 16

Scripture: Luke 2:6-7; James 4:1-10

The digs were humble at best. A "no vacancy" sign and a barn and a feeding trough. He came in to a world that thought it had no room for him. He came, not in a palace as a king, but in a manger as hayseed He was born in a stable to parents who were so uninfluential that they could not convince their way into a real hotel room.

The king of the universe, the maker of the stars, the One by and through whom all things have their being, took his first breath in a humility that no one saw coming. A humility that, to be honest, is unsettling and difficult to acknowledge, because we are not quite sure what to do with it. Tim Keller says, "The problem is that it takes great humility to understand humility." The king in a manger is bigger than we want to admit. Born in a manger and killed on a tree, this man would take his first breath and his last breath and all of the ones in between in a humility that we can hardly begin to understand.

The stable is the place to dig deeply into this humility. In our confusion and inability to understand, James says he gives more grace. The humble one gives us more grace than we could ever need to tread the waters of what feels unattainable. He gives us the grace to look around: at our lives and our homes and under our trees. He gives us the grace to deal with what we will find as we put on the lenses of humility. And, as we dive into the stable, he will draw nearer to us.

Prayer:

> *Lord Jesus, teach me to be generous. Teach me to serve you as you deserve, To give and not to count the cost, To fight and not to heed the wounds, To toil and not to seek for rest, To labor and not to seek reward, Except that of knowing that I do your will. Amen.*
>
> -St. Ignatius of Loyola

Day 17

Scripture: Luke 2:6-7; Ephesians 2:1-11

The humility of the birth of the King is not an idea I want to move from too quickly this season. I want to stay in this picture, the inn and the "no vacancy sign," the unimpressive back-up barn and the trough for a bed. The inn with a room for every head to lay but the three people who, in different ways, would fill the night with the cries of hope and rescue. As a child, I struggled with the idea that the King had been mistreated, his parents ignored and discarded. I heard stories of a tender innkeeper who made living quarters in a stable. However, the innkeeper in these conjectures did not feel tender to me. He felt smug or aloof and misinformed, but never tender. He could have afforded to move someone to make way for a King. If he had only known.

The more I learn of Jesus, the more the picture of his birthplace starts to make sense. Of course it was a humble place, a place for servants and animals and food and waste, not the place for a king. The more I learn of Jesus the more I understand that he could afford to be born in a barn. My friend Linds is in seminary, and one of her professors, a man called Hans Bayer, speaks often of humility. He explains that humility is the idea that we can afford to let others be the best version of themselves, and this, in turn, makes us the best version of ourselves. The idea changed my life. Humility is the idea that I can afford to let others shine.

Jesus was born in a barn and laid in a manger for more reasons than I could imagine. But I do know that the place matters. God is far too sovereign to be pushed aside by the smug innkeeper that lived in my childhood imagination. In this moment and in this season, the humility of his birth is a reminder that the King could afford to let others have a place to lay their head.

I want to be more like Jesus. I want to change in deep ways this season, in ways that make me understand that I can afford to let others...

Prayer:

> *Deliver me, O Jesus, from the desire of being loved, from the desire of being extolled or honored or praised or preferred. From the desires of being consulted, approved, popular. Deliver me from the fear of being humiliated, despised, forgotten, wronged or ridiculed. From the fear that others may be loved more than I; instead, Jesus, grant me the grace that I might desire it. That I might desire for others might be more esteemed than I. The desire that others may increase and I may decrease. That they may be chosen and I set aside, them praised and I unnoticed. That others may become holier than me, but that you would make me as holy as I should be. Amen.*
>
> -adapted from a prayer by Mother Theresa

Day 18

Scripture: Luke 2:8-9; Psalm 8:1-9

I remember my first time riding on an airplane. I was maybe 8 years old. I remember arguing my way to a window seat and sitting with my eyes glued to it, terrified of missing anything. When we made our way through a giant group of thick and puffy cumulus clouds, I dreamed of what they would feel like and promised myself that I would touch them one day. "One day" came when my friend Chris was getting his pilot's license. He surprised me one afternoon with the easiest question anyone has ever asked me, "Want to touch a cloud today?"

We flew the tiniest airplane thousands of feet in the air through a ceiling of stratus clouds. Finally the wispy clouds broke and I saw something I will always struggle to find words to describe. It was as if when the clouds broke, the heavens were exposed, declaring the glory of the Holy. We could see miles and miles. It was just Chris and I and the tiniest plane and the sky and the sun and some giant fluffy clouds. And I had a hard time catching my breath. And I was terrified. So genuinely afraid at the vast and the light and glory. Chris smiled so wide and nodded at me to open my window. We stuck our hands out the tiny cracks as far as we could reach them and giggled like children as we tried to grab the cold wisps of cloud. As if we were trying to catch the Holy.

The Celtic Christians talk about moments in life when the veil between heaven and earth is so thin it seems as if they are pouring into each other. This. This was a thin moment.

There were Shepherds standing in an ordinary field on an ordinary day, doing their ordinary jobs. In a matter of seconds, the clouds broke and the heavens were exposed in one of the most thin moments any human throughout history would ever experience. And heaven and earth for these moments felt like they were the same. Majestic and terrifying.

Prayer:

> *Oh, you are good, though, I almost missed it. I was looking to others to find my worth and my importance. But you drew me near to your sanctuary and showed me the big picture. Those who are far from you, they perish. But for me, I have found it is good to be near to you. You are what I desire on this earth. Though my heart and my flesh will fail, you are my refuge, my strength, my portion forever. Amen.*
>
> -adapted from Psalm 73

Day 19

Scripture: Luke 2:8-14; Galatians 4:4-5

For unto you is born this day in the City of David a Savior, who is Christ the Lord.

It was the birth announcement of the King. In a field full of shepherds he was announced and given the title above every title: Savior. Lord. Christ.

They couldn't have known. There was so much happening: their fear and surprise and the giant Warriors of Light announcing and praising and worshiping. They could not have grasped the magnitude of this moment.

The title that will one day be the final word. That at this baby's very name, every knee will bow and every tongue will call him by his title, Christ. Lord. (Philippians 2) This baby was their rescue. (Galatians 4) The one who would be the peace they had been searching for their entire lives. (Micah 5) This child would fill all of the gaps in all of history. In fact, his birth would be the most pivotal moment of all time. From this moment on, everything would be "before" or "after."

They couldn't have known.

This baby, He was the King.

Prayer:

Come, Thou long expected Jesus,
Born to set Thy people free.
From our fears and sins release us,
Let us find our rest in Thee.
Israel's Strength and Consolation,
Hope of all the earth Thou art.
Dear Desire of every nation,
Joy of every longing heart.
Born Thy people to deliver.
Born a child and yet a King.
Born to reign in us forever,
Now Thy gracious kingdom bring.
By Thine own eternal Spirit,
Rule in all our hearts alone.
By Thine all sufficient merit,
Raise us to Thy glorious throne.
Amen.

-from "Come Thou Long Expected Jesus" by Charles Wesley

Day 20

Scripture: Luke 2: 15-20; Micah 5:2-5

At church recently we were mid-communion. The lights were low and the song was sweet and something flashing caught my eye to the right. It was Megan, the daughter of some of my dearest friends, waiting in line for her first communion. A few days earlier, she called me with a secret, "Miss Lindsay, I have something to tell you. I asked Jesus to save me."

So there she was, waiting in line. Coming to the table for the first time waving a glow stick in the air. I don't know where the glowstick came from, but she had it and she was waving it. I watched her in line: her unruly curls, her skirt twisted just barely to the side, missing front teeth evident from her giant smile. Waiting and hoping and wondering what it would be like. She came to the table just as she was. Glowstick and all.

I wept in my seat as I watched Megan's dad, beaming proud and tender. I watched as he held her hand in line until they got to the communion station. When it was their turn, he did not fix her skirt or her hair or take her glowstick away. He just stood next to his toothless little girl and showed her how to dip the cracker into the juice, whispering its significance into her ear. His smile stretched his face as they returned to their seat, one of his proudest moments.

That night in Bethlehem, shepherds left their field and

fled to the stable. Often thought of as thieves and liars, shepherds had no clout, no gifts, nothing to offer. But still they ran, just as they were, to the feet of the King. To bow before his throne, dirty and covered in sheep.

Oh that we might approach the King in the same way, just as we are. With the confidence that there is room in the stable for the dirty and for the liars. Might we run toward the King, waving our glow sticks, waiting and hoping and wondering what will be.

Prayer:

> *O God, You never go away from us, yet we have difficulty in returning to You. Come, Lord, stir us up and call us back. Kindle and seize us. Be our fire and our sweetness. Let us love. Let us run. Amen.*
>
> -St. Augustine

Day 21

Scripture: Luke 2:19

Stories say that the dying words of Rabbi Abraham Joshua Heschel were, "Never once in my life did I ask God for success or wisdom or power or fame. I asked for wonder, and he gave it to me."

This life will offer you plenty of chances to run. The question is only: how fast and far and long can you go? The season is upon us and the days are full. There are things to be purchased and packaged and prepared at every turn. This season will give you every excuse you have ever needed to run, hard and fast and long.

But nothing about the Nativity makes sense. The incarnation of the King flips everything upside down.

There will always be a chance to run. There will always be busy. But this season is yours for the taking. And it is full of wonder and magic and something to treasure at every turn. You will not accidentally happen upon the wonder, the traditions, the magic. You must take a breath and slow your pace, for the moments of this season are yours to live or to miss. It is never too late for wonder.

> *It will be up to us to prepare for the Night of the Child, to prepare the way of the Lord, to make straight the paths. It will be up to us to make a journey of sorts toward Bethlehem, to spend some time listening to the story as it weaves its way*

through Advent. We are the ones who must make room in our hearts for the story to speak, who must listen carefully to its twists and its turns, listening for the places where it begins to tell us our own story.

-Ruth Haley Barton

Prayer:

Slow me down. Teach me to wait when I want to run. To be still when there are a million things to do. Give me wonder. The wonder to find you in the tiny moments I might have missed. Wonder to let those moments change me. Slow me down, O God, for the King is coming. Amen.

Day 22

Scripture: Matthew 2:1-12

These men, they did not fit in. The wise men were from the east, finding their wisdom in the stars. They were Gentiles, not the chosen of God. Not the ones waiting for a King. No, they were from the east and they were waiting on a star.

The angels declared that this baby was for all people.

And so they came from the east, following the star they had been waiting on and found the child. The child that would tear down the barriers of race and tradition and history. The child that was for everyone, everywhere.

The story of Christmas is for all of us. The dirty shepherds and the kingly wise men. The ones who have it all together and the ones who only have a thread. It is for those of us who are sure and those with questions. This story is for to broken, the bothered, the hurried, the sick, the tired, the uneasy, the confident, the brave, the wimpy. It is for those of us with too many traditions to count and those who just put up a tree this morning. This story, it is the story for all people. It is our story.

The king is here…

Prayer:

I was an outcast, a slave, a rebel, but your cross has brought me near and has softened my heart...O that I might love you as you love me. Amen.

-Valley of Vision

Day 23

Scripture: Revelation 21:3-7

I need to know that this baby is the Immanuel. That God is with us, created to dwell with us and to make us his people. With us in the mighty and the majestic, the sparkling lights and the tastes so extravagant they never leave our brains. With us in the good gifts that this season is full of. And in the same breath, I need to know that Immanuel is not something temporary. And that dwelling does not give him any clause to leave.

Because things are not always good, even in the merriest of seasons.

I need to know that God is with us in the good things and the sad things. With us in the empty plate and empty chair and empty fridge. God with us in the shadow and the question and the shame. God with us in broken dreams and broken homes and broken hearts. God with us in the lonely in a crowded room and the lonely in an easy chair, no one around. With us when the silence speaks too loudly and in the loud we try with all we have to tune out. With us when everything falls apart.

The bible declares Jesus' dwelling over and over again. It says he is with us and he is for us. And, that He is making all things new. Sally Lloyd-Jones, the author of the Jesus Storybook Bible, talks in her book about the "secret rescue plan" that God has created to buy back his children. She borrows a phrase from Tolkien that says that this rescue plan will make "all of the sad things come untrue." Some days, I need someone to yell it from the rooftops.

This Child came to be with you. He is the rescue and he came for you, in the sad and impossible, the wonderful and the adventure. He is with you. And, in him, all of the sad and all of the lonely and all of the death and hurt and despair will one day be untrue. For He is True King and he is making all things new.

Prayer:

All glory be to Christ our king!
All glory be to Christ!
His rule and reign we'll ever sing,
All glory be to Christ!
When on the day the great I Am,
The faithful and the true,
The Lamb who was for sinners slain
Is making all things new.
Behold our God shall live with us,
And be our steadfast light.
And we shall ere his people be,
All glory be to Christ!

-from "All Glory Be to Christ" by Derek Kensrue

Day 24

Scripture: Hebrews 11:32-40, 12:1-2

This Fall was a very difficult season of life. It felt like I was swimming in the ocean, barely able to touch and trying to keep my nose above the water. And then, just as my feet would touch the ground, another wave would come with fury and would knock me back under, filling my nose and mouth and eyes with water, salty and dry. Many days I would wake up and all I could do was breathe. In and out. In and out. And brace myself for the waves that never seemed to break or end. And then, I would swim with all that I had.

> *"Ooh!" said Susan, "I'd thought he was a man. Is he—quite safe? I shall feel rather nervous about meeting a lion."*
>
> *"That you will, dearie, and no mistake," said Mrs. Beaver; "if there's anyone who can appear before Aslan without their knees knocking, they're either braver than most or else just silly."*
>
> *"Then he isn't safe?" said Lucy.*
>
> *"Safe?" said Mr. Beaver; "don't you hear what Mrs. Beaver tells you? Who said anything about safe? 'course he isn't safe. But he's good. He's the King, I tell you."*
>
> *"I'm longing to see him," said Peter, "even if I do feel frightened when it comes to the point."*
>
> -"The Lion, the Witch and the Wardrobe" by C.S. Lewis

The King in the manger came that God might give us something better. His coming began the process of putting it all back together. But today and some days the broken is far easier to see and to feel. Theologians call this tension the Already and the Not Yet. The birth and death of Jesus mean that the Kingdom of God has "already" come. And the reality is that the Kingdom of God has "not yet" come in fullness.

So for now, we live in the tension. The tension is a hard and a sweet place to be. Thank God for the stories of the strong. And thank God for the stories of the weak and the incomplete. And thank God for the King, who is never safe and always good, who authored and perfected this faith and is with us all the while. Because He is good. He's the king, I tell you.

Prayer:

> *The troubles of my heart are tearing me apart. How I need Your saving hand to grant me a new start. Lonely and afraid, I call upon Your name. Save me from my enemies and cover all my shame. I will lift my eyes from this fragile life, for you will rescue me. I lift up my soul to you who makes things whole. Oh, mercy love of old, in you I place my hope. So guide me in Your truth, be my strong refuge. Oh, forgive my doubting heart and lead me back to You. Help me to believe, Your love is all I need and that even when the storm is strong, you will provide for me. Even in my darkest place, there's a promise I will claim: Those whose hope is in Your grace, they will never be ashamed. In you I place my hope. Amen.*
>
> -from the song "I Place My Hope" by Ellie Bannister & Ben Bannister, based on Psalm 25

Day 25

Scripture: Matthew 1:18-25

A young girl and her fiancée, on an ordinary trip to Bethlehem. When suddenly it was time, and the waves of pain got closer and closer together until the night became anything but ordinary to them. And the night that had been so quiet no longer was. And her cries pierced the air of the town full of lonely hearts and longing souls, people waiting for healing and for rescue and for a king. She lay on the cold hard ground, without a mother to sing comfort over her, holding the hand of a man she barely knew. The hand of a man whose obedience she could trust. A man who looked an awful lot like his unborn son, full of grace and mercy and hope. And he held her hand and timed her breaths, the mess and the beauty of labor filling his hands and bed like a symbol of his own heart. In a cycle of hope and of pain, earth stood still and waited for Love to be born.

This night, Love was born.

Love that swims into every crevice of your heart. Love that chose a teenage girl and a kind boy...and kings and whores and slaves and murderers and priests and weirdos. Love that blew air into your lungs. Love that knows your depths and still chooses you. Love that lays you bare on the cold hard ground and calls you by your name.

This night, my son. This night, my daughter. I was coming for you. I will always come for you.

Prayer:

The night feels so familiar, almost as if I was there. I remember this King. I can feel the silence and the chill and the waiting. And some days it feels like I have been waiting forever. Help me believe in what happened on this night over 2,000 years ago. Help me believe in the Love that came. The Love that makes all things new, even me. The Love that changes everything, even me. Might I leave this season, broken and bare, mended by the Love that calls my name. Amen.

Day 26

Scripture: Isaiah 61

> *At the center of the Story, there is a baby. Every story in the bible whispers his name. He is like the missing piece in a puzzle—the piece that makes all the other pieces fit together, and suddenly you can see a beautiful picture. And this is no ordinary baby. This is the Child upon whom everything would depend.*
>
> -The Jesus Storybook Bible

Sometimes when my bible opens it immediately falls to page 1352, Isaiah 61. The page is full of underlining and names and wrinkles. Full of memories and hopes. I think maybe they are the greatest words ever written.

Jesus, the baby upon whom everything would depend. The Immanuel who came to be with and to rescue the poor, the brokenhearted, the captive, the bound. The Savior who would to flip things inside out and upside down: gladness instead of mourning and beauty in the place of ashes. The Messiah, who came to redeem and restore the places in us and on this earth that have been long devastated.

And on a quiet night in a regular town, in a dirty stable he came. No trumpets blared. No luscious robes were brought in. He came into a town and a world that never saw it coming. That quiet night in the dirty stable was just beginning. He took the world by storm and He changed everything.

And on another quiet night on a dirty hill, the Savior, the Messiah, the King completed His rescue. So that one day, this King will come again for us. The King, who will make all of the sad things become untrue. The King, who will put everything back together. The King who loves you just as you are, not as you should be. The King who made a way, He will return for his people.

The King is coming...

Prayer:

Jesus, I belong to you, body and soul. Let it happen as you say. Amen.

Soundtrack

An eclectic mix of songs to help along the way.

- "Snow" by Sleeping At Last
- "All Glory Be To Christ" by Kings Kaleidoscope
- "Christmas Lights" by Coldplay
- "God With Us" by All Sons & Daughters
- "Baby Boy" for King and Country
- "Come and Stand Amazed" by Citizens
- "I Place My Hope" by Ellie Holcomb
- "The Earth Stood Still" by Future of Forestry
- "Hark the Herald Angels Sing" by Seabird
- "Little Drummer Boy" by For King and Country
- "Winter Song" by Sara Bareilles and Ingrid Michaelson
- "Come Thou Long Expected Jesus" by Kings Kaleidoscope
- "The Good Night Is Still Everywhere" by Derek Kensrue
- "Unto Us" by Folk Angel
- "Angels We Have Heard on High" by For King and Country
- "I Thank God" by the Avett Brothers
- "Rebel Jesus" by the Wood Brothers
- "Away in a Manger" by EmmyLou Harris
- "Winter Trees" by The Staves
- "Have Yourself a Merry Little Christmas" by Drew Holcomb + the Neighbors
- "Mary's Prayer" by Ed Cash, Bebo Norman & Allen Levi

- "Oh Holy Night" by Ed Cash, Bebo Norman & Allen Levi
- "Jesus, Oh What a Wonderful Child" by Ed Cash, Bebo Norman & Allen Levi
- "Born to Bleed" by Ed Cash, Bebo Norman & Allen Levi
- "Love Has Come" by Amy Grant
- "All the Poor and Powerless" by All Sons & Daughters

*Listen for free on Spotify from any computer: go.maryvillevineyard.com/advent